SCIENCE ANSWERS

Grouping Materials

FROM GOLD TO WOOL

Heinemann Library
Chicago, Illinois

Carol Ballard

Design: Jo Hinton-Malivoire and
 Tinstar Design Ltd (www.tinstar.co.uk)
Illustrations: Jeff Edwards
Picture Research: Rosie Garai
 and Liz Eddison
Originated by Dot Gradations Ltd.
Printed in China by Wing King Tong

08 07 06 05 04
10 9 8 7 6 5 4 3 2 1

**Library of Congress Cataloging-in-
Publication Data**
Ballard, Carol.
  Grouping materials: from gold to wool /
Carol Ballard.
      v. cm. -- (Science answers)
Includes bibliographical references and
index.
Contents: What are materials? -- Where do
materials come from? -- How are materials
made? -- Why are certain materials used? --
When are strong materials needed? --
When is waterproofing important? -- Why
do some materials keep you warmer than
others? -- What kinds of materials are rocks
and soils?
  ISBN 1-4034-0952-8 (HC), 1-4034-3549-9
(pbk.)
  1. Materials--Juvenile literature. [1.
Materials.] I. Title. II.
Series.
 TA403.2.B35 2003
 620.1'1--dc21
                    2003002504

Acknowledgments
The author and publishers are grateful to
the following for permission to reproduce
copyright material:

pp. 4, 5, 14, 15, 26 Liz Eddison; pp. 7, 12,
22 Photodisk; p. 8 Neil Rabinowitz/Corbis;
pp. 9, 13, 16, 18, 20, 23, 27 Trevor Clifford;
p. 10 Joseph Sohm/Corbis;; p. 11 Paul A.
Souders/Corbis; p. 17 Patrick
Bennett/Corbis; p. 19 Bob Krist/Corbis;
p. 24 James A. Sugar/Corbis; p. 25 Kevin R.
Morris/Corbis; p. 28 (bottom) Hulton
Archive; p. 28 (top) Hulton
Archive/Engraving by W. G. Jackman; p. 29
R. E. Litchfield/Science Photo Library; p. 31
Tudor Photography.

Cover photograph reproduced with
permission of Tudor Photography.

Every effort has been made to contact
copyright holders of any material
reproduced in this book. Any omissions
will be rectified in subsequent printings if
notice is given to the publishers.

Some words are shown in
bold, **like this.** You can find
out what they mean by
looking in the glossary

Contents

About the experiments and demonstrations

In each chapter of this book you will find a section called Science Answers. It describes an experiment or demonstration that you can try yourself. There are some simple safety rules to follow when doing an experiment:

- Ask an adult to help with any cutting using a sharp knife.
- Electrical sockets are dangerous. Never, ever try to experiment with them.
- Do not use any of your experimental **materials** near an electrical socket.

Materials you will use

Most of the experiments and demonstrations in this book can be done with objects you can find in your own home. A few will need items you can buy from a hardware store. You will also need paper and a pencil to record your results.

What Are Materials?

Materials are what make up other things. People use different materials to make different things.

Some common materials are stone, wood, glass, cotton, and china. Think about one of these materials. Can you write a list of words to describe what it is like? For glass, you might write *breakable, hard,* **waterproof,** and **transparent.** These are the **properties** of the material.

Materials all around you

Every day you use things made of many different materials. You might use a toothbrush made from plastic, a shirt made from cotton, a sweater made from wool, a plate made from china, a spoon made from metal, a chair made from wood, a lunchbox made from plastic, and a window made from glass. A different material has been used to make each of these things.

Using metals

Gold, silver, copper, aluminum, and iron are all metals. They are all alike in some ways: They are strong, they can be polished, they can be shaped, and they can be sharpened. Metals can be used to make knives and forks, suits of armor, jewelry, bicycle wheels, and much more.

If you were to compare two materials, they may have some properties that are the same. For example, stone and china are both hard and **opaque.** They may have other properties that are different. Stone is strong, but china is fragile. You can put materials together into groups so that all the materials in a group have some similar properties. Materials such as wool, cotton, polyester, and nylon can all be made into **fabrics.** They are all **flexible** and can be cut, stitched, and dyed to make a complete range of different clothes. Slate, marble, granite, and chalk are all types of stone. Teak, pine, mahogany, and balsa are all types of wood.

Where Do Materials Come From?

Some **materials** come from under the ground, some from animals, and some from plants. These are all natural materials. Some natural materials can be changed to make other materials.

Which materials come from the ground?

Some materials are buried deep beneath the earth's surface and have to be dug out from deep mines. Others are near the surface of the earth and can be dug out more easily.

Many different types of stone can be dug out from hillsides. Stone is often used for building. It can also be used for other things such as statues and gravestones.

Metals are usually found mixed with other things. These mixtures are called **ores.** Gold is unusual because it is not mixed with other things. It is found in pure lumps called **nuggets.**

Gemstones

Gemstones such as diamonds, rubies, sapphires, and emeralds are dug out of the ground, too. They are found as rough lumps, which are cut and polished so they sparkle in jewelry.

6

Woolly coats

Sheep and some other animals such as goats have thick coats of wool. When sheep are **sheared,** the wool is collected and spun into threads. Their coats of wool can be woven into a soft, warm fabric.

Which materials come from animals?

Animals provide some very useful and important materials.

Silkworms spin fine threads of silk to make their cocoons. People weave these threads into a beautiful, soft **fabric.**

Leather comes from the skins of animals such as cows. The skins are treated with special chemicals and may be dyed to change the color. Leather can be used to make soft, **flexible** shoes, jackets, and bags.

People have used animal bones, horns, and tusks for thousands of years. People use them to make musical instruments, ornaments, tools, weapons, and many other things.

Which materials come from plants?

When trees are cut down, people use the wood from the trunks and branches for building or making a variety of things such as furniture, musical instruments, and ornaments.

People harvest seed pods from cotton plants and then clean and spin the **fibers** inside them into cotton threads. People use these threads to make **fabrics.** They spin and weave threads from the flax plant to make linen.

Some plants such as willow have long, thin branches that people cut and lay out to dry. These are called canes and they are used to make baskets and furniture.

Many plants have brightly colored flowers, leaves, and berries. These can be squashed, which causes juice to ooze out. This juice can be collected and used to make dyes that are used to color things.

Rubber trees

Rubber trees produce a sticky juice called **sap.** Collected sap is used to make bouncy balls, car tires, and elastic.

DEMONSTRATION: How to make your own material dye

You can collect your own dye and color a piece of **fabric** by following the steps below.

EQUIPMENT

Some berries (Check with an adult before you choose your berries. Some are poisonous. Blackberries, blueberries, raspberries, and strawberries are all good to use.); two plastic bowls; a potato masher or fork; thin material such as cheesecloth or muslin; a rubber band; a white handkerchief or piece of fabric

DEMONSTRATION STEPS

1. Place the berries in one of the bowls.
2. Mash them with the potato masher or fork until they are completely broken into a pulp. (If it is really dry, you may need to add a little water.)
3. Stretch the cheesecloth or muslin over the other bowl and secure it with the rubber band.
4. Carefully pour the pulp onto the material and let it drip through into the bowl.
5. Throw away the material and pulp.
6. The bowl should contain a colored liquid.
7. Dip your white fabric into the liquid. Remove it and allow it to dry.
8. Rinse the fabric under running water. Does the color rinse away?
9. Write down what you saw.

EXPLANATION

You can make natural dyes from berries.

How Are Materials Made?

Many of the **materials** around you have been made by changing natural materials into something else. These new materials are called human-made or **manufactured** materials. Paper, glass, plastic, and paint are some manufactured materials.

How is paper made?

Paper is made from wood. People chop down trees and transport the trunks to a saw mill. The trunks are sawed into tiny pieces and then mixed with chemicals to make a slush called pulp. Sometimes, **bleach** is mixed with the pulp to make it white. Then the pulp is poured on to a flat screen, which is like a giant sieve, to let the water drain out. The pulp is pressed to squash out any water that is left, and then dried. When the paper is removed from the screen, it is ready to be cut into smaller pieces for use.

How is glass made?

Glass is made from two basic materials—sand and limestone. When these are heated together, they change and make a new material known as glass. Bottles, vases, and ornaments can be shaped by blowing air into hot, molten glass. Sometimes, other materials are added to the mixture to make special types of glass. Lead may be added to make fine glass for wine glasses. Other chemicals can be added to make colored glass or to make the glass stronger or heatproof.

How are new metals made?

Mixing two or more metals together can make a new metallic material called an alloy. Brass is made by mixing copper and zinc. It looks like gold but is much cheaper. Mixing aluminum with other metals produces light, strong alloys that are ideal for making bicycle frames and airplane shells. Adding other metals to steel can make even stronger alloys for making tools such as hammers, wrenches, and screwdrivers.

Where does plastic come from?

Nearly every plastic is made from chemicals that come originally from oil. At an oil refinery, oil is separated into many different chemicals. The chemicals needed to make plastics are removed.

Some plastics can be pulled into long, thin threads and woven into **fabrics** for clothing. They can also be used to make strong ropes, yacht sails, and parachutes.

Some plastics can be stretched into very thin sheets to make food wrap and other plastic wrappings.

Plastics all around

Dyes can be added to plastics to make every color of the rainbow! Some plastics can be **molded** into shapes to make things such as toys and garden furniture. Air blown into plastic gives it special shapes for bottles for drinks and other liquids.

DEMONSTRATION: Make your own plastic

You can make a plastic **material** from milk by following the steps below.

EQUIPMENT
One cup of full fat milk or cream, a saucepan or microwavable bowl, four to five tablespoons of vinegar, a plastic bowl, a piece of muslin or cheesecloth, a rubber band, a spoon for stirring, a stove or microwave oven

DEMONSTRATION STEPS
1. Ask an adult to help you pour the milk into the saucepan or microwavable bowl and heat it gently.
2. When the milk is hot, but not boiling, add the vinegar.
3. Stir the mixture well. It should start to thicken and become lumpy.
4. Leave it to cool for a few minutes.
5. Stretch the muslin or cheesecloth over the plastic bowl and secure it with the rubber band. Pour the warm mixture onto the fabric. The liquid should drip through into the bowl.
6. Squeeze all the rubbery material left behind into a ball.
7. Wash the ball under cold water.
8. Allow it to dry for a couple of days. Soon you'll have a ball of your own homemade plastic!
9. Write down what you saw.

EXPLANATION
The vinegar reacted with a substance in the milk called casein. This type of plastic is used to make many products including buttons, beads, and jewelry.

Why Are Certain Materials Used?

When you want to choose a **material** to make something, you need to think about the **properties** it must have, such as its hardness, strength, stretchiness, **transparency, flexibility,** ability to be **waterproof,** and much more.

Hard or soft ?

To make some things you need to use a hard material, but for other things you need a soft material. Look at the furniture in your house. A desk needs to be hard so that you can put things on it. Wood, metal, and some plastics are all hard, so they are all good materials for making a desk. A cushion needs to be soft so that it is comfortable to sit on. **Foam** and feathers are both soft, so they are good materials for filling a cushion.

Does it carry electricity?

Electricity can travel through some materials but not others. Materials that electricity can travel through are called electrical **conductors.** Materials that electricity cannot travel through are called electrical **insulators.** Metals and some ceramics are good electrical conductors. These are used for the centers of electric cables, to carry the electricity from one place to another. Plastics are good electrical insulators. They are used for the outside of cables, plugs, and sockets to prevent the electricity from leaving the metal center and causing damage or injury.

Flexible or rigid?

Can you imagine how uncomfortable you would be if all your clothes were stiff? Old suits of armor were made of metal, but they had a lot of joints so that the wearer could move around. **Flexible** materials such as **fabric** and some plastics are used to make things that need to bend and change shape, such as clothing. Other things such as walls and doors, bridges, bicycles, and airplanes need to be made from **rigid** materials such as stone, concrete, and metal so they do not bend.

INVESTIGATION: Find out if some elastic bands stretch more than others.

EQUIPMENT

A selection of rubber bands (some should be of equal length but different thicknesses and some should be the same thickness, but different lengths); a 12-inch (30-centimeter) ruler, a paper clip, and an object you can hang on the clip

INVESTIGATION STEPS

1. Hold the ruler vertically with the 1 at the top.
2. Hold a rubber band by one end on the 1 at the top of the ruler. Write the number that the other end (the bottom) of the rubber band reaches down to.
3. Slide the paper clip onto the bottom of the band. Attach your object to the paper clip.
4. Hold the band as in Step 2 and write the number the band stretches to.
5. Do the math: number in Step 4 – number in Step 2 = number of inches the rubber band stretched.
6. Repeat for all your rubber bands.
7. Write your results.

CONCLUSION

Some rubber bands stretch more than others, even if they are the same length. A thicker rubber band will not stretch as much as a thinner one that is the same length.

When Are Strong Materials Needed?

If you see a house being built, you'll see some strong **materials** being used. Walls are often built out of stone or brick. These are very strong materials and can support the weight of the roof and the rest of the building. Another strong material used for building homes is wood. Other structures such as bridges and skyscrapers also have to be strong. These are often built using materials such as a strong steel framework covered with large concrete panels.

Protective materials

You wear protective clothing such as a bicycle helmet to avoid hurting yourself. This clothing has to be strong enough to stand up to a severe blow and yet light enough to wear comfortably. Most protective clothing like this is made of some type of plastic.

Cars and other vehicles need to be strong, too, to form a protective case around you as you travel. Most car bodies and airplanes are made of specially strengthened metals.

EXPERIMENT: Which types of paper are stronger than others?

HYPOTHESIS
Thicker, heavier paper will be stronger than thinner paper.

EQUIPMENT
Long strips of different types of paper (such as tissue paper, paper towels, writing paper, mailing paper, crêpe paper, wrapping paper), sticky tape, a small plastic bucket or pot with a handle, some weights (you can use wooden beads or plastic building blocks, but they all must be the same size)

EXPERIMENT STEPS
1. Cut strips of paper 1 inch (2 centimeters) wide and 4 inches (10 centimeters) long.
2. Fold the end of the first strip around the handle of the bucket and stick it in place with the sticky tape.
3. Hold your paper up and carefully add weights one at a time.
4. Record how many weights the paper held before it broke.
5. Repeat with each type of paper.

CONCLUSION
Some types of paper are stronger than others. Can you see a pattern in your results? Are thick papers stronger than thinner ones?

When Is Waterproofing Important?

It is important that things that hold water, such as buckets, bathtubs, and bottles, are **waterproof.** Many **materials** are waterproof and can be used for these things. Metals and pottery were used for many years, but plastic is becoming more and more common. It is cheaper and easier to **mold** and can be made in a wide range of colors.

Warm and dry

Other things that need to be waterproof are things that keep water out, such as raincoats, boots, and umbrellas. Some are made of plastic, or **fabric** that has been coated with plastic. Some special materials, such as Gore-Tex, have been developed for waterproof clothing. These let water vapor escape, so you do not get hot and sweaty. But they do not let water in, so you stay dry and comfortable.

EXPERIMENT: Which material is most waterproof?

HYPOTHESIS
Plastic materials will be more **waterproof** than **fabrics** and papers.

EQUIPMENT
Different materials to test, such as polyethylene (plastic grocery bag), fabric, brown paper, and tissue paper; a plastic container; a rubber band; water; an eyedropper, pipette, or drinking straw; a stopwatch or watch with a second hand; scissors

EXPERIMENT STEPS
1. Cut a piece of each material bigger than the top of the plastic container.
2. Put a piece of material over the top of the container and hold it in place with the rubber band.
3. Carefully add five drops of water to the center of the material.
4. Time how long it takes for the water to go through the material and into the container.
5. Record your results.
6. Repeat with each material.

CONCLUSION
Polyethylene and other plastics are waterproof. The water just sits on the surface. Some materials, such as cotton fabrics, soak up some of the water. Others let the water pass through.

Why Do Some Materials Keep You Warmer Than Others?

Heat passes through some **materials** more easily than it passes through others. Materials that heat passes through easily are called heat **conductors.** Materials that heat cannot pass through easily are called heat **insulators.**

Trapping heat in homes

Building materials such as brick, wood, and glass are good heat conductors. This means that in cold winters, heat will escape from inside a house! To keep the heat trapped inside, builders use heat insulators. Air is a good heat insulator, so builders often use double-glazed windows. These have a barrier of air between the layers of glass. This helps keep the house warm.

New houses often have a layer of thick padding between two brick layers to trap the heat. Older houses can have a plastic **foam** squirted between the brick layers. The foam expands and fills the **cavity,** trapping the heat inside.

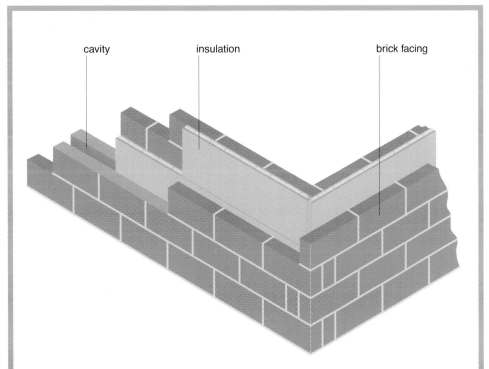

cavity   insulation   brick facing

Keeping your body warm

You need to keep your body warm, too. Air is a good heat **insulator,** so you often feel warmer with several thin layers of clothes—such as an undershirt, shirt, and sweater—than you do in one very thick sweater. This is because air gets trapped between the layers.

Some clothes, like ski suits, are made up of several layers. An outer **waterproof** layer prevents water from entering. Below it is a space that traps air. At the center is a thick layer of padding that is a good heat insulator. Next comes another space for air and an inner lining layer of cotton for comfort. This keeps the skier really snug!

Cool picnics

Heat insulators prevent heat from passing through them in both directions. So they are good at keeping things cold, too. The same sort of layered structure is used to make coolers for picnics.

EXPERIMENT: Which material is the best heat insulator?

HYPOTHESIS

The best heat insulators are those **materials** that can trap air, because air is a good insulator.

EQUIPMENT

Four identical plastic containers, four different materials for testing (such as a towel, aluminum foil, bubble wrap, paper towel), eight rubber bands, hot water (ask an adult to help you with this), a thermometer

EXPERIMENT STEPS

1. Wrap each container in one layer of one of your materials. Hold it in place with a rubber band.
2. Measure the temperature of your hot water.
3. Half-fill each container with hot water.
4. Leave the containers for fifteen minutes.
5. Measure the temperature of the water in each container.
6. Write down your results.
7. Subtract the number in Step 5 from the starting temperature to find out the drop in temperature in each container.

CONCLUSION

Some materials are better heat insulators than others. The best heat insulator is the material that was wrapped around the container with the smallest drop in temperature.

What Kinds of Materials Are Rocks and Soils?

The surface of the earth is made of rock. In many places, the rock is covered by soil or water, so you cannot see it. There are many different types of rocks, made in different ways.

Some rocks, such as chalk and limestone, were made from the shells and bones of sea creatures that died millions and millions of years ago. These shells and bones were crushed together under the sea and buried beneath many layers of mud.

These rocks can change when they are heated and crushed below the surface of the earth. New rocks are formed that are different from the original rocks. Marble is formed in this way from limestone.

Some rocks were formed below the surface of the earth. Here it is so hot, the rocks melt. As this molten rock rises to the surface, it cools and forms very hard rock such as granite. If it reaches the surface very quickly, perhaps when a volcano erupts, bubbles of gas are trapped inside. The gas bubbles create holes in the molten rock. This is how rock with many holes, such as pumice, is formed.

People use rocks and stones for buildings and other structures. If you look at an old building, you may see signs that it has been damaged over the years. Rocks can be damaged by the weather and other processes. This damage is called **weathering.**

Weathering rock

Weathering does not just happen to rocks that are used for buildings. It happens to bare rocks on hills, mountains, and sea cliffs and in deserts, too. Underground caves are carved out of rocks as water drips through and wears them away.

What is in soil?

Soil contains a mixture of different things. The biggest bits are usually small pieces of rocks and pebbles. There are also tiny pieces of broken-down rock called clay and often grains of sand. Most soil contains bits of dead plants and animals and animal droppings as well. When this dead **material** breaks down it is called **humus,** and it contains a lot of chemicals that plants need to grow well. **Microorganisms** help break up the humus and release the chemicals. Some small creatures, such as worms and beetles, live in soil, too.

Looking at soil

You can see what is in soil by taking some and putting it in a jar with some water. If it is shaken and then left to stand, it will slowly settle into separate layers.

EXPERIMENT: Why does water drain more quickly through some soils than others?

HYPOTHESIS
Soils with humus and other bits of matter will allow water to drain more quickly than soils without humus.

EQUIPMENT
A funnel; filter paper or cotton; a plastic container; soil samples from different places, such as from under a tree or near a pond, flower bed, or compost pile (ask an adult before you dig!); a plastic scoop or spoon; water, a one-cup measuring cup; a stopwatch or watch with a second hand

EXPERIMENT STEPS
1. Place the filter paper or cotton in the funnel and stand the funnel in the plastic container.
2. Add the first soil to your filter (count how many scoop- or spoonfuls you put in).
3. Add one cup of water to the top of your soil.
4. Wait for the water to stop dripping through the funnel into the container.
5. Record how long it took for the water to drain through.
6. Repeat with each soil.

CONCLUSION
Water does drain more quickly through some soils than others. Usually soil with a lot of humus will drain more quickly than soil that contains only a little humus.

People Who Found the Answers

Charles Goodyear (1800-1860)

Charles Goodyear, an American inventor, wanted to find a way to treat rubber so that it would not be sticky when hot and hard when cold. In 1839, he accidentally spilled a mixture of rubber and sulphur onto a hot stove—and this gave him a clue about how to improve the rubber. He had discovered that adding sulphur made the rubber stronger. He called his new process vulcanization. It was very successful and is still used for treating rubber today.

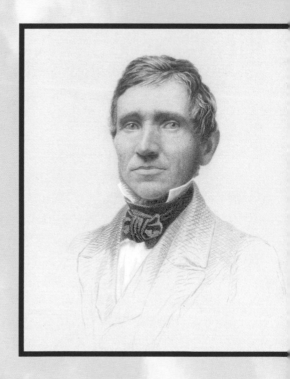

Leo Baekeland (1863-1944)

Leo Baekeland was a Belgian scientist who lived in America. He wanted to make a new type of plastic. Eventually he managed to develop a plastic he called Bakelite. It was the first thermosetting plastic, which is soft and can be **molded** when hot. But once set, it does not change shape, even if it is reheated. Bakelite became very popular and was soon used to make many household things such as door handles, telephones, and radios. Bakelite could be made in many colors, so it was also used to make jewelry. Because many people now collect Bakelite jewelry, it has become very valuable.

Amazing Facts

- Diamonds are made from the same stuff as the graphite in many pencil leads! They are both made of a chemical called carbon. All that is different between the two **materials** is the way in which the tiny carbon particles are held together.

- Do you have a fleece jacket to keep you warm in cold weather? Can you guess what it is made from? Believe it or not, it's probably made from recycled plastic bottles! It's amazing to think that bottles can be melted down and changed into that lovely soft, snug material!

- A diamond is not just a pretty stone to put into jewelry. It is the hardest material in the world. It can cut through anything at all, even glass and rock. Many machines that are used for cutting and drilling use diamonds.

- Nylon is a human-made **fiber** that is used in many types of clothing. It was invented by scientists working in both New York and London. They did not know what to call this new **fabric,** so they took the letters of their cities and put them together: *New York LON*don

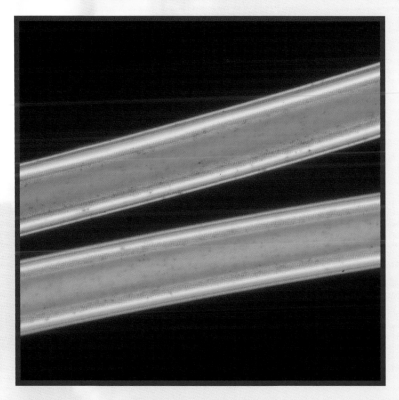

Glossary

bleach   chemical used to make a fabric white or colorless

cavity   hole in a solid object, such as a wall

conductor   material that lets electricity pass through it. A heat conductor lets heat pass through it.

fabric   material made of threads woven together

fiber   long, thin thread

flexibility   how much a material can bend

flexible   able to bend easily

foam   light, spongy material used for insulation and packing

humus   pieces of dead plants and animals found in soil that has been broken down by microorganisms

insulator   substance that does not let electricity pass through it. A heat insulator does not let heat pass through it.

manufactured   made or produced in a mechanical way

material   what something is made from

microorganism   very tiny living thing that can be seen only with a microscope

mold   form into a required shape

nugget   lump of pure gold

opaque   cannot be seen through. A stone wall is opaque.

ore   metal mixed with other things in the ground

property   characteristic of a material. A property of stone is that it is strong.

rigid   stiff and not flexible

sap   fluid found inside a plant

shear   cut wool off a sheep

transparency   how see-through something is

transparent   see-through. Glass is transparent.

waterproof does not let water pass through it

weathering wearing away of rock by the weather

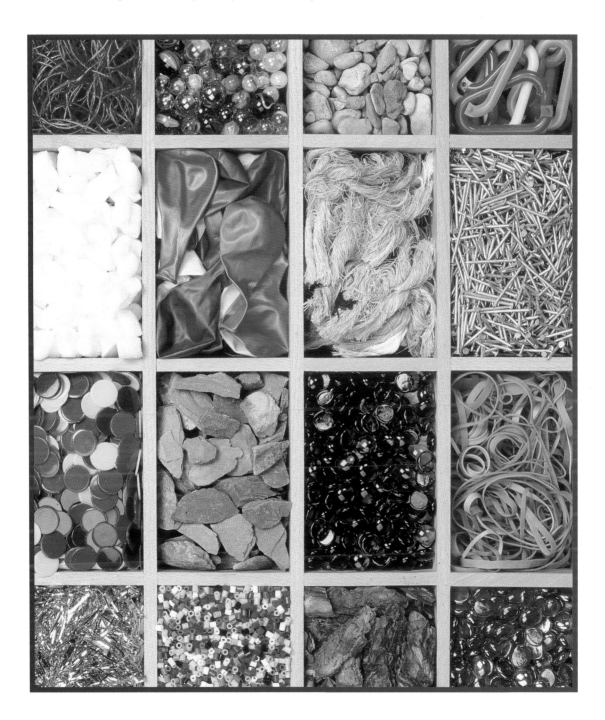

▶• Index

▶• More Books to Read

Bigham, Julia. *The 60s: The Plastic Age.* Milwaukee, Wis.: Gareth Stevens, 2000.

Snedden, Robert. *Materials All Around Us: Changing Materials.* Chicago: Heinemann Library, 2001.